GHOSTS 3

CAUGHT ON FILM

GHOSTS 3

CAUGHT ON FILM

PHOTOGRAPHS OF THE SUPERNATURAL   GORDON RUTTER

D&C
David and Charles

A DAVID & CHARLES BOOK
Copyright © David & Charles Limited 2011

David & Charles is an imprint of F&W International, LTD
Brunel House, Forde Close, Newton Abbot,
TQ12 4PU, UK

F&W Media International, LTD is a subsidiary of F+W Media, Inc.,
4700 East Galbraith Road
Cincinnati OH45236, USA

First published in the UK in 2011
First published in the US in 2011

Text copyright © Gordon Rutter 2011
Photographs copyright © see page 159

Gordon Rutter has asserted his right to be identified as author of this work
in accordance with the Copyright, Designs and Patents Act, 1988.

A catalogue record for this book is available from the British Library.

ISBN-13: 978-0-7153-3903-9 hardback
ISBN-10: 0-7153-3903-6 hardback

10 9 8 7 6 5 4 3 2 1

Printed in China by Toppan Leefung Printing Limited
for F&W Media International, LTD
Brunel House, Forde Close, Newton Abbot, TQ12 4PU, UK

Commissioning Editor: Neil Baber
Editor: Sarah Callard
Proofreader: Cheryl Brown
Senior Designer: Victoria Marks
Production Controller: Kelly Smith

F+W Media publish high quality books on a wide range of subjects.
For more great book ideas visit:

www.rubooks.co.uk

Contents

INTRODUCTION

THE WORLD'S MOST HAUNTED CITY?

A Cathedral With a Ghostly Priest
Craigmillar Castle Kitchen Orbs
Haunted Hotel
Portrait Phantom
Watched From a Window Ghost
Reflective Ghost in the Vaults
Women in White in Black Mausoleum
Plague Doctor Still Checking on His Patients

GHOSTS ON THE MOVE – MOBILE PHONE PHOTOGRAPHS

Are You a Ghost Fan?
A Pub With Spirits
A Skull in the Living Room
Sleepy Old Man in the Woods
An Extra Playmate
The Spirits of Brazil
Virtually a Ghost
Still Watching the Television
Dog and Orbs

Introduction

Ghosts, if they exist at all, are not easy to see. If they were, then everyone would have had a ghost sighting or have a ghost story to tell. As it is, if you ask your friends, some will have such a story but the majority will not. This is particularly so if we talk about, to use the phrase from the film *Ghostbusters*, 'a full body apparition', in other words, a full-on visible ghost. Therefore, if ghosts are not easy to see it follows that photographs of ghosts must be rarer still. How many of us actually have a camera ready at a crucial moment – any crucial moment not just the appearance of a ghost?

Ever since the first photographs were taken in the 1820s (by the French inventor Nicéphore Niépce, who, interestingly destroyed his early attempts saying their appearance was too ghostly), there has been a stream of photographs purporting to depict ghosts. Some of these images have been covered in previous volumes in this series and some are now iconic. Now, in the 21st century, the rules of the game are changing. Today it is difficult to go anywhere in a major city without being photographed by CCTV. Many people also carry some sort of camera with them most of the time. Digital compact cameras are to be found everywhere and with no developing costs and instant results they are being used more and more. Mobile phones routinely have cameras as a basic accessory. And, courtesy of a wide range of popular television shows, people are more interested in ghosts than they have been probably since the Victorian period. So, shouldn't new ghost photographs be surfacing – fresh images to keep the ghost debate raging? The good news is that of course there are. However, the problem is getting to see these images as many are locked away in family photo albums or passed between only small groups of friends.

The aim of this book is to give some more recent and less well-known ghost photographs the airing they deserve. But how do you go about collecting photographs that are family possessions and have never been published before? Simple. You ask people. And that's what has happened here. During 2008, Richard Wiseman, Caroline Watt, Alison Rutter and I were sitting around chatting. Richard had come up with the idea of a one-day conference, as part of the world-famous Edinburgh International Science Festival, to look at hauntings and the science of ghosts.

We all thought this was a good idea and over even more wine our plans began to take shape. As part of the event we would have a website where people could submit their own photographs and discussion and voting could take place. At the conference we would then announce the photographs that were voted the most likely to be a ghost. I would give a talk on the winners and a brief summary of the history of photography. Having been interested in both photography and the paranormal for the past 35 years, it was a combination of two of my hobbies – how could I not be excited about such a project. Simon Gage, director of the Science Festival,

liked the idea and so it was go. Some of the submitted photographs are included here, so thank you to those who agreed their pictures could be used and thank you also to everyone who submitted an image (over 300 people).

However, not all the pictures came from the *Hauntings: the Science of Ghosts* event at the Science Festival. In the course of giving lectures on the paranormal, people often mention to me that they have a photograph that they think a bit strange. Would I be interested in seeing it? Of course I would! Sometimes pictures are just passed on to me out of the blue as people hear about my interests. In these days of cheap computers and digital cameras though, image manipulation is both relatively easy and very possible. There is also the chance that people may simply be mistaken about what they are looking at; the human brain is very good at putting together random shapes and coming up with a face. Some of these photographs are genuine conundrums though.

One thing I decided whilst writing this book was to take the photographers at face value. Most of the images came with a story of the circumstances they were taken in and some of these can be readily checked. When a digital photograph is taken, data about the image is recorded and embedded in it. This information can be read with the appropriate software; the file produced is an EXIFF or metadata file and it can tell you such delights as the camera settings used (e.g. shutter speed, aperture setting, or whether the flash was used) and even the make and model of the camera. This can be very useful in explaining what is seen in the photography and specific examples of this are included in the text where relevant. However, it is inevitable that some photographs here are deliberate fakes, where the individual concerned has intended to catch people out and to deceive. This is a shame but it is the way things are. I have met some of the photographers in person and in a couple of cases they have confessed how their fakery was achieved. Any photograph that is not as described initially by the photographer is labelled as such. So that leaves the rest – genuine people with a genuine story and perhaps a genuine ghost photograph?

In terms of selecting photographs for each chapter, there are a number that could have been placed in several chapters. For example, if we have a picture of a headless ghost in Edinburgh Castle taken on a mobile phone of someone's birthday party, we have an image that would comfortably fit in almost every one! I've tried to place photographs of this nature where I feel it is most natural for them to appear.

And of course, new ghost photographs are still appearing. If you have one that you'd like to send, I can be reached through my website at www.gordonrutter.com.

Enjoy the book and don't be afraid to take photographs! You never know what might appear on them.

The World's Most Haunted City?

Many unbiased sources list Scotland's capital city, Edinburgh, as one of the most haunted in the world – and it's not difficult to see why. It's an ancient city, the oldest extant building is some 1,000 years old, and a castle dominates the skyline, along with an extinct volcano and other volcanic remains. The city has felt the full ravages of war and plague – each several times over.

The unique design of Edinburgh means that historic buildings have been buried under new developments creating an 'underground city' of cellars and dwellings. There are also the stories of murderers such as Burke and Hare, body snatchers turned serial killers who, as digging up graves and exhuming corpses was too much like hard work, murdered their victims and sold the bodies to a local doctor. Even some of the world's most famous literary ghosts have their origins in

Edinburgh – Charles Dickens was inspired to write *A Christmas Carol* when he was walking through Greyfriars Kirkyard (cemetery). And that's not to mention the horrific witch trials that took place, often resulting in the burning of unfortunate individuals who were most probably guilty of nothing more than arguing with the wrong person.

Edinburgh has embraced its past and long association with ghosts and the paranormal. A whole tourist industry has built up around its ghostly past and there are shops selling paranormal paraphernalia, and several underground streets and vaults hold ghost tours. Every year the city hosts a ghost festival called the Edinburgh Ghost Fest and at Halloween and May Day there are re-creations of pagan festivals.

As I was compiling this book it came as a surprise to see that time and again there were photographs from Edinburgh. This was by no means deliberate, requested or particularly sought after. But nevertheless, it is welcome. The pictures represented in this section include traditional haunted locations such as churches and castles but also such seemingly innocent places including guesthouses and hotels. Despite taking many photographs in my own Edinburgh home and the surrounding area, I regret to say that I've never captured a ghost. However, with a wealth of photographs from Edinburgh, perhaps it truly is the world's most haunted city after all?

A Cathedral With a Ghostly Priest

St Giles Cathedral is a major landmark on the Royal Mile and a popular location for photographers. This image was taken on a dull and overcast day just at the right moment – that is, when no one else was around and likely to wander into the photograph – so giving an uninterrupted view of the subject.

In low-light situations it's always best to take several photographs to increase the chance of getting a good one (particularly with digital cameras as it doesn't cost any extra). And that is what happened here.

On the right-hand side in the second tier of seats is the clear image of a priest

This was the middle of three photographs taken in rapid succession whilst the photographer's mother watched. On the right-hand side in the second tier of seats is the clear image of a priest. Both individuals are certain that no one was present at the time. Also, it should be stressed that this was the middle of three shots with only a few seconds between each. If someone had moved into shot and then moved out again, they would have been noticed or perhaps even caught in the act on one of the other photographs.

A possible explanation is that the area of missing chairs causes our brains to fill in the details of a figure; or perhaps it is a coat left over a chair or even the result of the shiny chair backs reflecting light towards the photographer.

The World's Most Haunted City?

Craigmillar Castle Kitchen Orbs

Here we have the kitchen area of Craigmillar Castle. The two photographs are taken just a couple of seconds apart, yet one is full of orbs and the other has none. For the sake of discussion, let us say orbs are paranormal in nature – if so, why did they all choose to leave the area of the photograph at exactly the same time? I do not know of a paranormal explanation for this effect, but there is a non-paranormal one.

Believers in orbs point to the fact that when orbs are enlarged, faces can be discerned in them and are different between orbs. If the non-paranormal theory that orbs are small objects such as dust or pollen is true, we have an explanation for these differences. Dust and pollen particles are not all identical and as such, reflections from them and images including them will be different.

...when orbs are enlarged, faces can be discerned in them and are different between orbs

As the person has walked to the kitchen area, dust that is too small to be seen with the naked eye has been stirred up. The first photograph is taken and the flash illuminates the orbs. The second photograph is taken a few seconds later during which time the air currents have changed the position of the orbs. They are most likely to have been flowing into the space vacated by the individual as she walked, i.e. essentially following her. As such the orbs have moved and are now closer to the subject. There is only a narrow space in which dust and particles will be perfectly positioned to give the orb appearance and by the time of the second picture they have moved away from this zone. Therefore, orbs that are different to each other are seen in the first picture but vanish in the second.

15

Haunted Hotel

A group of friends were staying in Edinburgh and while the rest of them made plans for the night ahead, one stayed in the room to get ready. She decided to take a few photographs of the room as a memento. After the trip the photos were processed and on viewing them they saw something unexpected in this picture. The image of a woman can be seen in the window. The room in question is on the first floor (or second floor for any American readers) so it can't be someone walking past – unless they're on stilts!

The photographer was alone in the room and it's not her reflection as she is blonde and the figure is dark haired, these are not the clothes she was wearing and her camera cannot be seen. The figure is wearing a white maid's cap, but this photograph was taken just before the group went out for the evening, so there shouldn't have been any maids around – particularly not outside the window of a first floor room.

The photographer was alone in the room and it's not her reflection as she is blonde and the figure is dark haired

The figure appears to be either reflected in the window or on the other side of the window rather than superimposed over it or between the photographer and the window. If it's a reflected person, painting or television, then these objects would have to be very large indeed. An impressive and intriguing picture.

Portrait Phantom

A family visit to the city's number one tourist attraction, Edinburgh Castle, offers a great photo opportunity. When this image was downloaded onto a computer an aberration was discovered. The portrait of King Charles II has what appears to be, according to the photographer, a ghostly image of a woman standing next to the king with her hands on his shoulders.

It does indeed look as described, and with a squint of the eye there is even a suggestion of a ruff around her neck. Alternatively, it also looks like the classic 'wailing sheet' type of ghost.

As we look at the picture there is more illumination on the left-hand side. This suggests that a flash has been used for the photograph (as indeed many galleries have low illumination to preserve the paintings). The portrait appears to be varnished and what seems to have happened is that some light has reflected from the picture to give us this aberration. Indeed the photographer seems to have been aware of this possibility and has positioned themselves slightly to the left of the picture to try to counteract this effect.

...a ghostly image of a woman standing next to the king with her hands on his shoulders

Watched From a Window Ghost

Another visit to Edinburgh produced this ghostly image. This particular photograph is from a rented flat some 300 years old. During the last evening of the couple's stay the lights went out. Rather than moan about it they decided to use the opportunity to take a photograph of the view of the rest of the city showing the illuminated flats nearby. The picture was taken and when the preview screen of the camera was viewed there was a slight blurriness in the bottom corner, so the picture was taken again with exactly the same result. There was no additional light other than those of the flats and when the window was examined there were no smudges, drying marks or anything similar found.

Upon seeing the picture clearly the photographer was a little 'freaked out'. One obvious suggestion would be a reflection of something within the room but surely the photographer would have noticed something such as a spooky statue? One problem with this picture is that the evidence seems to show a flash being used – we can see illumination of the curtains, window frame and outside vegetation. However, in the photographer's description they claim that no flash was used. If this were taken during a power cut with no lights, where has the illumination come from? The whole thing strikes me as rather suspicious.

Upon seeing the picture clearly the photographer was a little 'freaked out'

Reflective Ghost in the Vaults

An American tourist in the haunted vaults of Edinburgh (part of the ghost-based tourist industry) took various photographs on his tour. At the time he and members of his family felt and saw nothing untoward. It was not until their return to the USA when they had the film developed that they saw something unexpected on the photograph. At the end of the corridor there seems to be a little white figure, perhaps of a ghost in chains.

To add to the tour atmosphere, these areas are usually quite dark, so the illumination for the picture is from the flash. The effects of the flash can be seen by the brightness of the areas closest to the camera, with the light level falling off rapidly as the distance from the camera increases.

In this location it is alleged there is the ghost of a cobbler, so perhaps this figure is a cobbler with a white apron sitting and working on a shoe? If there were something reflecting the light, it would be visible to the photographer after the image had been taken, but there was nothing evident.

This is a curious one: there is a corridor to the side of the apparent image but no evidence of light coming from that area to illuminate anything (we would expect to see differential illumination somewhere else in that location). This was shot on film so there is no digital information. If there is a defect on the film it looks unlike any I've previously encountered. For me, assuming there is no fakery, this makes the photograph very interesting.

At the end of the corridor there seems to be a little white figure, perhaps of a ghost in chains

Women in White in Black Mausoleum

Greyfriars Kirkyard (cemetery) is most famous as the home of Greyfriars Bobby, a dog who supposedly remained at his master's grave, but more recently there have been alleged outbreaks of poltergeist and haunting activity.

This photograph (one of 240 taken on the night in question) was shot on a tour around the area. The tour went into an area that is usually locked, the Covenanters' Prison. Once in there, the normal tour destination is to go inside a tomb called the Black Mausoleum. This picture was taken on a mobile phone within the Black Mausoleum. At the right-hand side of the photograph we can see someone wearing a high-visibility jacket showing up in the torchlight that illuminates the scene. (A torch was used as the image was taken on a mobile phone without flash facility.)

Inside the mausoleum there are no windows and the only light is that which shines through the doorway. At the time the photograph was taken there were only two people in the vault, the photographer and subject, as the guide was waiting outside. However, to the left of the image there appears to be two cloaked and cowled figures, one large and one small. Subsequent to the photograph being taken, the photographer and her companion returned in the presence of a medium. The medium came up with the name Alice or Alison Greer. There is an Alison Grier who was buried in Greyfriars in 1685.

...there appears to be two cloaked and cowled figures, one large and one small

Plague Doctor Still Checking on His Patients?

This picture is, for me at least, unique. Of all the photographs in this book it's the only one where I was present as it was taken, on an evening ghost tour during the annual Edinburgh Ghost Fest, at The Real Mary King's Close, a visitor attraction in a warren of underground streets and spaces.

The room in question is an old cattle shed next to a re-creation of a room full of plague victims. The photographer was standing next to the plague room looking around when a moving light attracted his attention in the cattle shed. He pointed his camera in the direction and clicked. The light can still be seen on the left of the photograph – it's the back of my camera and the light is coming from the preview screen; I was the only person present in that part of the room. The photograph was just one of many taken by the photographer that night. Subsequently, he was going through the shots on his computer when he came across this one. At first he thought nothing of it, but when he got up for a cup of tea the different viewing angle made something leap out – the figure on the right-hand side. He boosted the light levels on the image to reveal a figure wearing what appears to be traditional plague doctors' dress. Whilst there are dummies in the museum dressed like this, there are none in that area. Is it a plague doctor who has come to check if the disease has run its course?

The room in question is next to a re-creation of a room full of plague victims

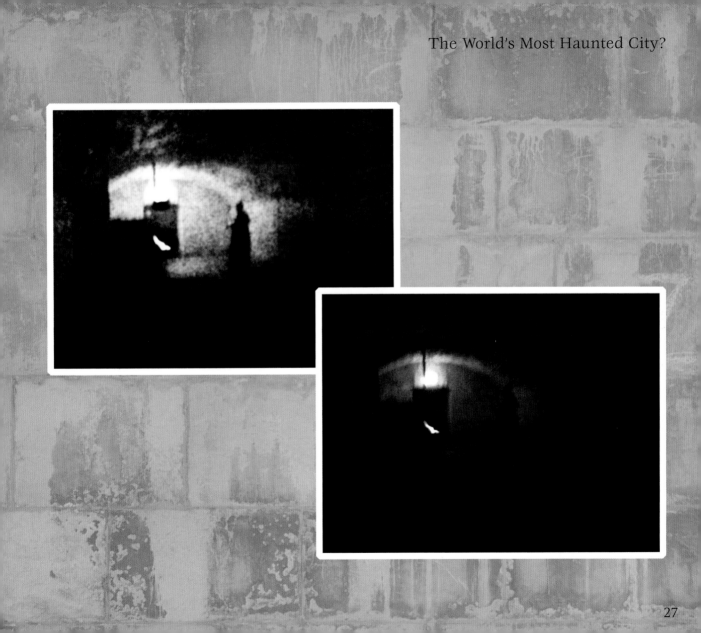

Ghosts on the Move – Mobile Phone Photographs

One of the greatest inventions of the late 20th century is the mobile phone (or perhaps it's one of the greatest nuisances ever created – opinion is still divided). Now in the 21st century it seems that finding a mobile phone without a camera is an almost impossible task. As a result many of us are carrying a camera with us at all times. This means that photographs are being taken anytime and everywhere.

Nearly 200 years after the invention of photography we are almost all equipped to take photographs wherever we go and whenever we want. This has resulted in more photographs being taken than ever before. One estimate puts the figure at 300 million digital photos per day. As a result, it would be surprising if people did not take photographs that gave pause for thought.

This chapter includes a number of images said to be photographed by a camera on a mobile phone, which are undoubtedly less reliable than a camera. Most people with any type of digital camera are familiar with the notion that more pixels give a better picture and, overall, the image-quality

of camera phones has improved many times over. Early camera phones gave images of (for example) 200,000 pixels but rapidly changing technology put 10,000,000 (10 mega pixel) cameras in our pockets. So, instead of an enlarged picture rapidly breaking into blocks of colour with no detail, images can now be enlarged to reveal details. For early camera phones it wasn't worth printing pictures as the quality would be so poor, but today enlargements from camera phones sit proudly on many mantelpieces.

However, the number of pixels is not the only feature of a camera that allows us to view detail; the lens is also critical. In many camera phones the lens is the weakest link. Sitting on the back of the camera they are often prone to being covered in dirt and fingerprints, or to being scratched – all of which will degrade the quality of the finished image. Additionally, many camera phone lenses are made of plastic, which is inferior to the glass used in dedicated cameras.

The majority of camera phones do not have a flash to provide additional light in dark conditions so photographs may be underexposed. People try to correct this by using software designed to improve visibility, but that also allows us to see noise in the photograph. This noise is a random firing of some of the sensors, making the picture grainy or dotty and introducing images that were not present as part of the original scene. The picture might also be blurred because to get the right amount of light the shutter has to stay open for a long time. Whilst the shutter is open the phone is not always held steady, so the result may be multiple images (a fault called, appropriately enough, ghosting).

As technology advances, the problems are fewer and the technical quality of images improves. However, there will always be a lag between the picture quality produced by a camera phone

compared to a dedicated camera, but this is not a surprise as cameras have never been great for making phone calls! All said, under the right conditions, it is possible to get excellent results with a camera phone. Examples of the possible pitfalls of using a camera phone can be seen in this section. However, don't let this put you off using one as it's better to have some photographic record of an event than none at all.

Are You a Ghost Fan?

Here is a low-resolution picture taken with an early mobile phone. The photograph was taken in a 110-year old house and is of something that was claimed to be visible at the time. The photographer moved out two weeks after taking the photograph. Others, who remain at the house, report that there are constant noises heard at night, noises they don't believe are caused by settling of the house.

The image looks to have been created by some sort of light anomaly but there are no obvious light sources. The picture was taken at 4am when no one else was awake, so it's unlikely to be someone shining a torch into the room. One thing is unclear – where the illumination is coming from. Is there a light on in the room? If so, it's not doing a good job of illuminating the room. This camera phone doesn't have a flash, so is the illuminated part of the room lit by the object? This photography raises many more questions than it resolves.

Others, who remain at the house, report that there are constant noises heard at night

A Pub With Spirits

This is an apparent camera-phone photograph that has been extensively lightened to produce the image we see. This is evident from the low resolution and high noise value – both resulting in an image that is very blocky with poor contrast. The photo was taken in a pub in Henley, Oxfordshire, and the photographer has done further research on the image and area and he has come up with the name Mary Blandy. He says that the more you zoom in on the figure in white, the more distant it becomes, and he adds that the hands of the figure look as though they are tied together. The photographer says he submitted the picture to the Institute of the Paranormal who agreed it was a strong image (I have been unable to track down the Institute of the Paranormal to verify this).

Mary Blandy was hanged in 1752 when she was 31 for the murder of her father

Mary Blandy was hanged in 1752 when she was 31 for the murder of her father. In life she lived near to the pub where this photograph was taken and there have been a couple of alleged sightings during the past 250 years.

Is this the ghost of Mary Blandy, hands bound on her way to the gallows? Or is it simply a girl walking in the background who happens to be wearing a dress that could be interpreted as old-fashioned?

A Skull in the Living Room

In this instance a new mobile phone is being used. The house is allegedly haunted – the owners believe the ghost appears three to five times a year and whenever it is present they feel a chill in the room and get very emotional. When the photograph was taken there was no one around other than the photographer and her husband and there was nothing on the glass door, but when they looked at the picture they saw the skull-like face reproduced here.

The phone in question does not have a flash, so there are no aberrant reflections. Also, the only light is the ambient light which helps to further explain the low image quality (many cameras struggle to produce good images in low-light levels and when computer software is used to boost the image it also boosts unwanted noise).

Some have suggested the face appears more like the stereotypical 'grey' alien rather than a ghost, but it seems most likely it is simply a combination of reflective surfaces (very rarely is window and door glass totally smooth), ambient light and low resolution, which gives the suggestion of a face.

...whenever it is present they feel a chill in the room and get very emotional

Sleepy Old Man in the Woods

The photographer was walking through a park that had previously been home to a monastery, when he paused to take a photograph of his friend with a mobile phone. When the photograph was examined they found two ghostly images. One is a female figure in the background to the middle right, and the other is a face – described by the photographer as a sleepy old man – that can be seen at the top of the picture between the friend and the apparent female ghost. The ghostly figure looks to be shambling towards the camera.

This is one of those photographs where sceptics are trying to have their cake and eat it by complaining the ghostly figure is too crisp and clear. They're not saying it's too clear in relation to the blur of the photography surround, just that the image is too easily seen for it to be a ghost! I suppose it makes a change from decrying pictures because they are too blurred to positively identify.

The ghostly figure looks to be shambling towards the camera

Certainly, we have all the classic characteristics of poor camera phone quality displayed here. The photographer admits the camera phone was a cheap one. The image edges are blurry with only the central part sharp – the ghostly image shows this same level of blur. The whole photograph appears relatively blocky as it has a low resolution on the sensor. All of these elements give an overall effect that makes it difficult to analyse.

An Extra Playmate

Here is a camera-phone image from a house that is alleged to be haunted. The owner says he often sees a small child aged three or four running past the lounge door, although no such child lives in the house.

When this photograph was taken there was a child present in the foreground, yet when we look at the picture we can see another child crouching between two of the standing figures. The owner of the image says this child was only seen when the picture was downloaded to their computer. The image appears to be of a small child grabbing hold of the two sets of legs and peering through them. The face is very clear and does not appear to correspond to background materials such as the skirting board; nor does it appear to be formed from any parts of the individuals present.

The child moved because she insisted that she was being pushed from behind

The child on the right of the picture, who is clearly distressed, was originally standing where the ghostly 'child' is. She moved because she insisted that she was being pushed from behind. At the time the adults thought she was just making a fuss and told her off, which led to the tears. The adults changed their minds in view of this picture.

So that's the story attached to the image but this photograph has appeared several times in paranormal circles, accompanied by similar stories, yet with different locations

The Spirits of Brazil

Shown here are two photographs taken on a mobile-phone camera in Brazil. The house is where the photographs' owner's father and grandfather were born and used to live. When the photographs were taken there were only two individuals in the house, the photographer and a friend, both young men. The family believe the pictures, although indistinct, show the father in white (who died 1981) and the grandfather in dark clothes (who died 1951). The person to whom the photographs belong was neither of the individuals present but is convinced of their integrity.

Some sceptics have suggested the reason there is a similarity with the two family members is that two cut out photographs of them were held in front of the camera.

It has also been suggested that the figure in white is just someone walking past in a dimly lit room creating a motion blur on the photo. Another explanation given is that the figure in dark clothing is actually an action figure – basically a toy doll.

The family believe the pictures show the father in white and the grandfather in dark clothes

Virtually a Ghost

The photograph shown here by Ian Simons is a deliberate fake. It has been made using a technique to produce ghost images that have been reproduced in newspapers and magazines as conclusive proof of the existence of ghosts. All that is required to replicate it is the appropriate Smartphone with camera function, plus the £0.99 application that can be downloaded from the App Store. The app will give you a menu of different ghostly figures that you can preview on screen. You can then arrange the image so the ghost is where you want it and all you have to do is take the picture. You can even control the transparency of the ghost!

The app will give you a menu of different ghostly figures that you can preview on screen

Here we have the picture both with and without the optional ghost – simple and quick. The only saving grace is that currently there are only a limited number of figures available to superimpose, so once you are familiar with those, you can easily dismiss them as potential spirits.

Still Watching the Television

This is a camera-phone photograph taken of a newly-purchased television. As with all phone cameras the screen is relatively small and it was not until the picture was viewed on a computer that the anomaly could be seen.

The ghostly figure is just to the right of the television with his chin level with the bottom of the screen. It appears to be a small boy looking towards the camera. He seems to be dressed and to have a haircut in the style of the mid-20th century, but I guess small-boy fashions don't change that much!

The ghostly figure to the right of the television appears to be a small boy

The figure is a little low for the apparent body size, as if he were standing on a floor at a different height. The sun is quite clearly shining into the room just above the figure's head and there are lens reflections on the left-hand side of the television.

On the extreme left of the photograph, on the shelving unit, there also seems to be the world's first photograph of a ghost plate! I think this is just an extension of the lens flare being enlarged by the effects of the internal lens elements, which, in a mobile phone, isn't of the highest quality.

As for the image of the small boy, the photographer admitted that to include the figure, the image was manipulated. It's easy to be taken in, so when viewing photographs of this nature we should always be open minded to the possibility of things being real, but we should also be sceptical – the evidence needs to be convincing.

Dog and Orbs

A mobile-phone picture of the photographer's daughter playing with the family dog is shown here. The owner of this photograph has taken many pictures containing orbs and is intrigued by them. As with standard orb pictures a flash has been used – clear evidence of this can be seen in the reflection on the fire surround in the background at the extreme left. This glare or reflection has nothing to do with the orbs seen here – the illumination must be close to the camera and, most importantly, only a very short distance from the lens.

This is one reason why orbs are more often seen with camera phones and compact digital cameras – an SLR has the flash further away from the lens axis and so is less likely to produce theses types of images.

As people move around in preparation for a photograph they disturb the air and this explains why small particles of dust are set in motion. Subsequent movement makes the particles move even more which explains why orbs can be present in one image but not the next – the dust particles have simply moved out of the zone where orb production is likely. However, there are still people who believe strongly that the presence of orbs in a photograph is evidence of paranormal activity.

...orbs are more often seen with camera phones and compact digital cameras

Orbs and Lights

Light anomalies on photographs are frequently interpreted as ghosts and of these, the most common are orbs. Orbs are a very contentious issue amongst photographers of the paranormal. For some, an orb always represents a ghost or spirit in the process of materialising and no matter how many times they are shown to be commonplace, the true believer will still not accept it.

Websites discussing orbs consider them to represent the last vestige of the human soul or life force. They describe how enlargement of orbs shows features such as the face of the person as they appeared in life. Some paranormal sites report that orbs are not spirits at all but merely random projections of ectoplasm (said to be the raw material of a materialised ghost) that have no consciousness or 'life energy'. So even believers can't agree on exactly what they are.

The non-paranormal explanation is that orbs are objects close to the camera lens illuminated by the flash as it fires. These objects include particles of dust and pollen. Some photographs of orbs have shown distinct colours and these can often be matched to the clothing worn by the people in the photo, suggesting that the orb is dust being formed from particles of clothing.

Because the particles are close to the camera they are bright and out of focus. Also, as they are small they are easily blown about by the slightest air current, and the orbs may be present in one picture and absent in the next a second or two later, due to random movement of air. And, let's be honest, many of the best ghost locations are very dusty.

Orbs are more frequently encountered with digital than film cameras because of the relative placement of the lens and flash, which are very close together in most digital cameras but this isn't the case with older, film cameras.

Ultimately, it's a judgement call; does the evidence convince you that orbs are paranormal or are you confident with the prosaic explanation? Here we have a series of orbs and orb-related (light anomaly) photographs. These range from apparent shining figures in the sky, interpreted as guardian angels, through to purple patches of light believed by some to be recently deceased relatives watching over them or ghosts of people associated with a particular area.

Within this category we also include mists, particularly when no one other than the photographer and their party was present when the photograph was taken. For a number of photographs here the flash used to illuminate the dark scene has a lot to answer for...

Former President's Orbs

After the election of Barrack Obama as American President there were a large number of celebratory parties, including this one in Atlanta, Georgia, attended by former President Jimmy Carter and his daughter Amy. The photographer took this and many other photographs, but was particularly moved by the presence of several orbs here – the most noticeable orb is immediately above the head of former President Carter.

This photograph was taken under the shelter of trees, providing dark conditions where pollen could be present and where a flash would need to be used. Also, it's an outdoor party – so there may have been a barbecue with soot and small particles of ash floating around.

...the most noticeable orb is immediately above the head of former President Carter

Christmas Orbs

The photographer who sent this picture started their description with a question: 'Is this an orb?' Yes it is, but an orb is not a ghost as has been previously discussed and illustrated. The story behind this image is typical of an orb photograph in that it is one of a series of pictures taken in rapid succession, yet this is the only one the orb shows up on.

The photograph was taken whilst Christmas presents were being opened and, if it is anything like it is in my house, this activity can be quite energetic, and, as a result, any dust in the area is easily kicked up into the air. As soon as some of it enters the 'Goldilocks zone' of orb production (close enough to the flash to be brightly illuminated and close enough to the lens to appear large and out of focus) you will get an orb.

'Is this an orb?' Yes it is, but an orb is not a ghost

The Goldilocks zone is narrow and once the dust moves from there, no more orbs are produced. Evidence of flash usage can be seen because the foreground is light and the background area rapidly fades into relative darkness.

My Guardian Angel

The photographer of this image says: 'This photo was taken on the day of my prom. There is nothing in my hand or anywhere near it that can account for the angel-like light in my hand.'

It's always interesting to see how different people interpret the same evidence. For some she is clearly holding a mobile phone or LED light on a key fob. For others it is lens flare – light bouncing around inside the camera lens reflecting off the multiple glass elements. Yet others see it as a processing fault – a kink in the film or a batch of too-old developer.

One of the most amusing explanations put forward is perhaps even more unlikely than a ghost. The suggestion is: 'The subject has been to a beauty salon and had her nails done. As the nails were painted a small diamond-shaped piece of glass was stuck on them. The nails were also intricately etched. So we have a reflection from the "diamond" and refraction from the close etched lines on the nails.' Simple really.

'There is nothing in my hand or anywhere near it that can account for the angel-like light in my hand'

More film-orientated individuals have even suggested, with tongue firmly in cheek I hope, that the subject is either ET attempting to phone home or a Jedi Master from *Star Wars*! Despite the subject clearly stating she has nothing in her hand there are some who will go to their graves believing she is holding a light of some sort. And then for some it will always be an angelic ghost.

The Angel, London

A late-night ghost walk in London's haunted Green Park is the location for this photograph. Images such as this can be produced from a wide range of sources. There is quite solid cloud cover over this part of London, an area which is also full of nightclubs. Many clubs use searchlights or lasers to put on a light show to attract business and when they shine on low cloud they can produce quite beautiful effects.

Another possibility is that it is a gap in the clouds, which just happens to be vaguely angel shaped. Think of the cloud shapes we see during the day – this is just a negative version of that with a bright light, such as a full moon perhaps, to illuminate the gap to create the effect of an angel watching over the group of ghost hunters.

...the effect of an angel watching over the group of ghost hunters

For some this explanation may sound a little laboured and they might prefer to believe it was a genuine angel. But it's not – it is the moon. I have the photographs taken immediately beforehand showing the full moon with clouds moving across it. And if that is not enough proof, I remember the clouds moving into position as I watched, and then I got my camera out and started photographing the scene. Yes, I took this picture, and it is possibly the closest I have come to taking a ghost photograph.

An Infrared Angel

Here we have a photograph of Bachelor's Grove Cemetery, Chicago, taken with infrared film in 2005. Infrared produces haunting or otherworldly images all by itself – colours are distorted, for example; grass and leaves usually appear white. Also, infrared films are normally fast-speed films so the resultant photographs are often grainy – the film equivalent of pixelation.

The large black object in the background is a gravestone and in front of it to the right there is an object that some viewers say resembles an angel (others have likened it to the robot R2D2 from *Star Wars*!).

Some of the background does seem visible through the image, suggesting it is not a gravestone reflecting infrared light. Also, the photographer is adamant there is no gravestone in that spot, although as the graveyard is reputedly haunted by moving gravestones, who knows!

...the graveyard is reputedly haunted by moving gravestones

There is a relatively clear definition of a face but due to the way infrared film operates, the majority of the image is incorrectly exposed (the normal light meter of a camera exposes for visible light so it gives an inaccurate reading for infrared; this can be compensated for but does not appear to have been the case in this instance). So there really isn't enough information to say exactly what we have here.

An Angelic Hug

The photographer doesn't think this is a ghost photograph, merely a happy accident of mist and light producing a classic Victorian-type spook, complete with arms enfolding the subject. You can almost hear the clink of Jacob Marley's chains as you're looking at it!

It's obviously a cold day, so the mist could be caused by condensation from the photographer's breath or something more substantial such as cigarette smoke. The mist/smoke is then illuminated by the flash, which gives it a glowing appearance. Of course there are some who claim it shows ghostly energies, and one person has even claimed it's a guardian angel.

The most likely explanation is mist from the photographer's breath or cigarette smoke, which was in just the right place when the photograph was taken.

However, with 300 million digital photographs taken per day it would be more amazing if some mists were not in the shape of an angel, a ghost, or even Elvis. An excellent photograph even if it's not a ghost.

You can almost hear the clink of Jacob Marley's chains as you're looking at it

Misty Pirate Skull

Here we have a photograph from a treasure hunter who is searching for the treasure of pirate Captain William Kidd. Having found an interesting cave at midnight he took a couple of photographs, the first showed an orb and the second is this one.

After taking this picture the camera stopped functioning and has never worked again. The photographer thinks it looks like a headless man, but I see a definite head amongst the mist with spider legs appearing from the side, somewhat reminiscent of the first alien appearance in the John Carpenter version of *The Thing*.

One viewer suggests it might be a cobweb illuminated by camera flash. If that were the case, it would have also appeared on the first photograph.

After taking this picture the camera stopped functioning and has never worked again

It is clear from the image that the cave interior is damp, so it may be that the water is in the process of evaporating and a mist has been produced which has been caught in the flash.

Alternatively, as the photograph was taken late at night, it could be very cold forcing the breath of the photographer to condense and produce a mist. The first mist-free photograph could have been taken immediately upon arrival at the cave mouth before the camera could catch any exhaled water vapour.

Misty Face and Cathedral

Palace Green is an open grassland area in front of the rather splendid Durham Cathedral and equally splendid Durham Castle in the northeast of England. The photographers were on their way to a concert in the cathedral and as they passed through the green, which was unusually quiet, they were moved to take a photograph on this clear and starry (and as it was February, presumably cold) night.

They took photographs of the cathedral and castle, both floodlit at that time. The pictures were subsequently viewed on a television screen (the photographers did not have a personal computer but did have the appropriate cables to attach the camera and television). They were amazed to see what appeared to be a face in front of the cathedral. The face is in the middle at the top.

They were amazed to see what appeared to be a face in front of the cathedral

From the view of the car roof it looks like there might be an elevated position for the photograph. Also, we can assume a flash has been fired because the image of the car and wall are light and correctly coloured. If the illumination was by street lamp alone there would be a colour cast, and we can see evidence of reflective highlights of the flash on the car.

Swimming Ghost

This picture is interpreted by the photographer as a purple ghost looking at her daughter. Here again is a digital photograph where the anomaly was not noted until the photographs were viewed at home – it is easier on a bigger screen after all.

Some have looked at this picture and described it as celestial energy, whereas the majority see a ray of light from the sun shining into the camera lens and bouncing around in the optics (lens flare). The specific colour could be due to the coating on the lens.

However, those who believe in the ghost aspect of this photograph refer to a local story about the area being haunted. The story goes that a boy had been out on the lake when his boat sprung a leak and he drowned whilst trying to swim ashore.

The ghost disappears before it reaches the safety of dry land

Allegedly, the boy was wearing a purple shirt at the time of his death. The ghost of the boy has supposedly been seen several times, but always over the water. The ghost disappears before it reaches the safety of dry land. Other sightings have been seen in the same area but other photographs taken at the same time from the same position do not show the anomaly. Oh, and just to add to the mystery – when you enlarge the top of the purple area it starts to show more of a face-like shape to it.

The Holy Ghost

This photograph was taken during a Christian meeting in Africa and the photographer advises that 'the Holy Spirit – the Spirit of God and the book of Acts, Chapter 2, Verses 1–4 provides more information'.

This part of the Bible states: 'And suddenly there came a sound from heaven as of a rushing mighty wind, and it filled all the house where they were sitting. And there appeared unto them cloven tongues like as of fire, and it sat upon each of them. And they were all filled with the Holy Ghost, and began to speak with other tongues, as the Spirit gave them utterance.'

I assume it is the 'cloven tongues like as of fire' that is being referred to and the photographer is drawing our attention to the streams of light coming from the top of everyone's heads – except they are not. Again we have here a low-light situation where the camera has fired the flash and the shutter has also remained open for a long time. Evidence of the flash is obvious – the people closest to the camera are correctly exposed (with one casting a very dense shadow) and as we retreat (particularly to the left of the picture) the light rapidly falls away. Proof of the long exposure is the tongues of flames themselves. These originate from the brightly illuminated screen to the right of the image. Once the flash has fired the camera has been moved to the right and the bright screen has been recorded. However, there are others who feel we are seeing the bright auras of the worshippers.

> *...the photographer is drawing our attention to the streams of light coming from the top of everyone's heads*

Ghost Caught in Cap

In this photograph, taken on a coach journey, the photographer points out the orange light upward and to the left of the boy's head. In this light they claim you can see the face of another young boy, wearing a cloth cap with its shadow clearly visible on the bridge of his nose.

As we can see from the light trails we have the night mode in operation – the visible lights, such as the ceiling light in the bus and the reflection on the drinks bottle, are all seen to follow a specific line – diagonally from right to left.

When we look at the placement of the boy wearing the light-coloured hat and the aberrant image we have the same line of movement between them. Again we have movement during the slow shutter speed of the exposure and it is this that gives the under-exposed translucent effect. As the flash has gone off the boy on the left has moved slightly, tipping his head into a different position, and this coupled with the different camera angle gives a nice example of this type of photograph.

In this light they claim you can see the face of another young boy

Location, Location, Location

For some ghosts location seems crucial – they wouldn't be caught dead anywhere else! Of the locations that seem the most ghost-productive, photographically speaking, are castles and palaces. There are many castles and palaces throughout the world and they all seem haunted to a greater or lesser degree. Possibly the only other type of building with a similar level of ghostliness are theatres. Unfortunately with theatres, you are generally discouraged from taking photographs, so there aren't many images of theatre ghosts. However, castles and palaces are another matter. When these locations are visited, photography is usually encouraged – these are buildings that are owned by people or organisations that are proud of them, and they're generally proud of their ghosts as well.

Castles and palaces are old and full of history, and often much of that history is steeped in blood, so it's not too surprising that stories of ghosts and hauntings abound. From Hampton Court with

its famous ghosts (although we have here a couple of new appearances) through to locations that have never shown any signs of a haunting until now, they're all here.

As well as castles and palaces there are other site-specific hauntings. For example, there is a photograph from a battlefield. If ghosts truly are spirits of the dead returned because they have unfinished business, what better place for a reappearance than a battlefield where plenty have been killed before their time, leaving undone the many things they would have wanted to do before meeting their natural end?

Another theory of ghosts is that of the 'stone tape'. This states that when emotions are released the energy that comes out with them can imprint itself on the very fabric of a building or physical landscape. Then, when the conditions are right the emotional energy is released – the recording is played back if you like – allowing us to see the individuals that were responsible for the imprinting as well as the events that led to it.

I've never been on a battlefield during a war, but it does not take great deductive powers to realise that emotions would be running high, so if the stone tape theory is correct, we have a prime location for a haunting.

Other settings appearing in this chapter include ghost hunt locations Since the boom in televised supernatural investigations started a few years ago, the number of investigative groups has grown out of all proportion. Part of the investigator's tool kit is a camera. One photograph here was taken on a ghost investigation, and after seeing it the investigators returned to check the location to see if they could find any logical explanations to account for the sighting. They couldn't.

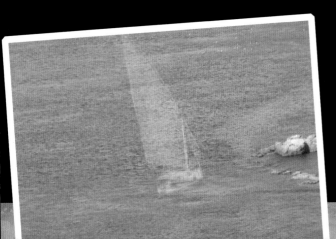

Finally, a couple of pictures here are not of ghosts in the traditional sense but are location specific. One is the unsettling ghost of the World Trade Centre Twin Towers and the other is of a phantom felucca (an Egyptian boat). Can non-living things have a ghost form?

Warwick Castle Ghost

Warwick Castle, a medieval castle in Warwick, England, is a popular tourist attraction. In the centre of this photograph we can see a window opening onto an area of the castle that is not accessible to the public, and in the middle there is a shape. The photographer is not convinced it's a ghost but is curious about it.

The most likely explanation appears to be a shadow caused by the crenellations and battlements along the top of the castle wall. However, like many of these photographs, when examined more closely, the centre of what would be the head area does appear lighter, giving the appearance of a face. It's possible there is a rock at just the right position that is catching some light, or is not in such dense shade, so that a paler, face-like appearance is visible. Unfortunately the resolution of the original image starts to pixelate before too much detail can be made out.

Another possibility is that the figure is a member of staff on a break – because although the area is not accessible to the public, it doesn't mean staff can't use it. But of course, as with all castles, there are stories of resident ghosts and in 2007 the castle opened a haunted dungeon attraction as part of its tourist experience.

...the centre of what would be the head area does appear lighter, giving the appearance of a face

Linlithgow Palace Ghost

In the large window to the left of this photograph of the ruins of Linlithgow Palace (West Lothian, Scotland) there appears to be a face standing proud of the brickwork, surrounded by a mist of some kind. The photographer notes the face is a completely different colour to the surrounding brickwork. Again this is a photograph where the person behind the camera was unsure what they had, so released it for others to see and comment on.

Linlithgow Palace has its traditional ghosts. There is the Blue Lady who is said to walk from the door of the palace to that of the adjacent church. Then there is the ghost of either Margaret Tudor (the wife of James IV of Scotland) or Mary of Guise (the wife of James V of Scotland), a figure often seen standing at the top of the tower waiting for her husband to return. Therefore, if this photo is one of these ghosts, they seem to be outside their normal haunt.

...there appears to be a face standing proud of the brickwork, surrounded by a mist of some kind

Some suggest the apparent face was an embossed piece of stonework sticking out and that the mist around it was simply weathering. The photographer was so intrigued that he returned to make sure the image wasn't due to a shield boss of some sort. He took photographs from exactly the same spot and no matter how much he blew them up, or how hard he looked, he could not find anything resembling a face or a boss at all.

Tantallon Castle Ghost

After people had seen the photograph from Tantallon Castle in the final chapter, this one emerged. It's a shot from the late 1970s and shows the owner of the photograph and her brother and father, the picture being taken by her mother.

The window above the father's head shows a figure that was not seen when the photograph was taken, only once the film was developed. This is the window above the one featured in the Tantallon picture that appears on page 157, taken 30 years later.

At first glance it looks like an image of the Elephant Man with the cap and cover he would wear when he went out. Some viewers think it looks very similar to the figure in the later photograph and one viewer claims a crown is visible on the figure's head!

Tantallon Castle is not one of the many castles worldwide that trades on its alleged hauntings, nor does it employ costumed guides. In fact it seems rather embarrassed by any potential haunting, which is a shame as we have two nice photographs here that may point to the presence of ghosts.

At first glance it looks like an image of the Elephant Man

Abandoned Mental Institution Ghost

Abandoned mental institutions, such as Whittingham Hospital in Preston, northeast England, are the perfect location for a possible ghost sighting. Since its closure in 1995, Whittingham Hospital has gained a reputation for being haunted and has hosted many informal ghost hunts. In fact, whilst it was still a working hospital some of the staff reported eerie goings-on, ranging from figures glimpsed from the corner of the eye to an entire corridor that gained a reputation as somewhere you didn't go if you could help it.

This particular photograph was taken through the remains of a wall. The bars that are clearly visible are part of the steel frame used to reinforce the concrete after much of it crumbled away. The camera was simply poked through a hole in the wall to photograph the room.

When the photographer came home from his excursion, he developed and printed the photographs; when he examined this one he thought he could make out a figure through the middle of the picture. With a head to the extreme left, there is a crown of black hair with eyes and nose visible, and in the centre part of the picture, the figure of an infant held in the arms of the adult. As a place of unimaginable anguish, is it possible a psychic imprint has been left there?

...is it possible a psychic imprint has been left there?

Battlefield Ghost

It is said that on the anniversary of the Battle of Naseby*, sounds, and in extreme cases sights, of the battle can be witnessed. It was this very claim that brought the Northampton Paranormal Group there in 2004. After a five-hour investigation there was nothing to report other than a few photographs of orbs. It wasn't until a couple of days later when one of the group members was checking through their photographs that they found this image. On the extreme right can be seen the Naseby ghost soldier and in the centre in the purple mist are two ghost horses.

The first point to notice is that this photograph was taken in the dark with a flash, as you can see that the foreground is illuminated. However, due to the strength of the flash there is only a small area that is correctly exposed. To see detail elsewhere the photograph has been lightened using photo-manipulation software. This doesn't mean an image has been added, but simply that what is there has been boosted.

On the extreme right can be seen the Naseby ghost soldier

Boosting light levels in this way begins to show random dots (pixels) that produce images – literally a do-to-dot scenario. There could have been background lights that moved during the exposure and we are merely filling in the details as we look at them.

*The Battle of Naseby took place on June 14, 1645. It was a bloody encounter in the English Civil War where the Royalist forces of King Charles I met with Thomas Fairfax and his Roundhead troops. The Royalists lost and this was essentially the beginning of their overall defeat. The Royalists lost 1,000 men and a further 5,000 were captured, while the triumphant Roundheads lost 400 men.

Twin Towers Ghost

This photograph was taken in New York in 2008. At the extreme left of the image are two faint towers in the position of the World Trade Centre Twin Towers that were destroyed in 2001. A traumatic event such as this may be expected to mark the psyche of people but is it enough to make a ghost of a building?

Unfortunately, this photograph won't answer that question, as I'm afraid it's a misidentification of the local geography. A careful examination shows that many famous buildings of the New York skyline are not where they should be. Chief amongst these is the Empire State Building to the right of the picture. The Twin Towers should be even further right for this view from New Jersey. Therefore, what we have are two other glass and steel towers that at first glance seem to be the Twin Towers but in reality is the Time Warner Centre constructed during 2001.

...can you have the ghost of a building?

However, the photograph does provoke an interesting discussion – can you have the ghost of a building? There are reports of ghostly carriages and even one of a ghostly London bus, and of course virtually all reported ghosts are said to be wearing clothing, so is this idea really so far fetched?

Former Amsterdam Orphanage Ghost

On a trip to a museum in Amsterdam the photographer decided to take a picture of her husband. Nothing unusual in that, and as can be seen from the photograph, it's not a shot at night, indoors or with a flash, so the picture is unlikely to be the result of a slow exposure. And yet, when we look over the shoulder of the subject we can see a faint image of a little girl on the upper landing. The photographer describes her as a young blonde girl with a pink top and white tights.

The figure does appear in great detail, perhaps too much for a trick of the light and the brain filling in the gaps. If it is a double exposure then what are the chances of the girl appearing in exactly the right spot where she would actually be able to stand?

So would we expect to see a ghost of a little girl in an Amsterdam museum? If ghosts exist it's as good a place as any, but when we look at the history of the museum we find that the Amsterdam Historical Museum used to be an orphanage. Other photographs were taken during the visit, including one where the husband photographed his wife sitting in the exact same spot, but none show anything anomalous. There is light shining through the trees, which can be seen to the side, but if that's the cause of the apparition then where are the colours coming from?

...we can see a faint image of a little girl on the upper landing

Skeletal Cardinal Wolsey at Hampton Court

The location is London's Hampton Court Palace, inside Cardinal Wolsey's rooms, on the other side of the palace from the famous Haunted Gallery. A photographer is taking a photograph of his friend looking at one of the many paintings on display, but it seems that she is about to have a surprise – a tap on her left shoulder from a ghostly hand, in fact a skeletal hand, reaching out from the skeleton that appears to be emerging from the left-hand painting.

...a tap on her left shoulder from a ghostly hand, in fact a skeletal hand

This photograph is easily explained though. The clue is in the exact shape and colour of the hand. It has a yellowish-orange cast. In photography, film and digital cameras are balanced to produce a white image under certain light conditions. (The default of the sun shining at noon in the UK will produce a white image of a white piece of paper.) Other lights have colour casts to them. For example, fluorescent tubes or energy-efficient bulbs will give a yellowish-green colour cast – the exact colour varies according to the make and age of the light. Here, if we look at the ceiling, we have a yellowish-orange light cast by the lights hidden at the top of the ceiling pointing upwards. Therefore, the hand is a reflection of the ceiling light and its skeletal appearance is simply the decoration on the ceiling.

Digital cameras have a built-in white-balance adjustment that normally changes automatically but where there is mixed lighting, the brightest light takes precedence. In this case the flash illuminating the subject is most dominant and the photograph is automatically balanced for that. It would appear that a glass panel in a door rather than a picture causes the reflection. Hampton Court may have more ghosts than you can shake an executioner's axe at but it appears that this is not one of them.

St Albans Ghost Hunt

Unlike many other photographs in this collection, this one was taken on a deliberate ghost-hunting expedition around the cathedral town of St Albans in southeast England. During the course of the evening various photographs were taken showing mists and orbs but this was the one the group felt was the most unusual and spooky.

The light starts in the background and appears to be quite low down, perhaps amongst a group of trees close to ground level. As stated by the photographer, it's not a street light nor is it a light illuminating the cathedral, which is reportedly haunted. The streaked exposure of the light implies it is an electric light powered by mains electricity. But what is providing the illumination?

During the course of the evening various photographs were taken showing mists and orbs

When faced with such situations people can be incredibly inventive in their reasoning as to what is shown. For example, one person seriously suggested the photograph showed a burning rope attached to the trees!

My feeling is that there was an artificial light – perhaps a motion-sensitive light? To solve this mystery, a daytime visit to the location would be helpful, to see what is there, if anything. If no light of any sort were found, it would produce an intriguing problem.

Kitchener's Felucca

Here is a view on the River Nile between Elephantine and Kitchener's Islands. The river is covered with feluccas (Egyptian boats). A digital photograph is taken and when the photographer checks the screen he sees a mist-like boat, fully transparent. Attempts to take a second, similar picture all fail. The obvious cry of double exposure is heard with a photograph of this nature but if that were the case why are there no waves relating to the boat? Perhaps it is taken through a pane of glass and we are seeing a reflection of a felucca behind the photographer?

The photographer thinks the image is a result of reflections and refractions from the water. But if it is a ghost, we have the intriguing idea that non-living objects can have ghosts.

...the felucca was smashed to pieces and the captain drowned

In the Aswan area of the Nile where the photograph was taken there is a local tradition relating to Lord Kitchener's felucca. Kitchener had been surveying the area and when he had time to relax, he would spend this on his felucca. On one occasion the felucca was being manoeuvred around some small waterfalls when disaster struck; the felucca was smashed to pieces and the captain drowned.

Shortly afterwards the villagers started to see a felucca appearing and disappearing in the water in the area. These sightings stopped when the Aswan Dam was completed, but recently the ghostly felucca has returned. The exact locations of the sightings are said to relate to the stability of the political situation in Egypt: upstream of the original cataract represents trouble coming, whilst downstream the problems are being resolved.

Soldier in France

A traditional, picturesque street photographed in the village of Grimaud in France: in the foreground, to the left of the picture is the photographer's wife, walking up the street; in the background an elderly couple are also walking up the street and the old woman appears to be looking directly at a dark figure or very dense shadow to the right-hand side of the picture. The photographer feels the image looks like a World War II soldier. Once he and his wife had noticed the anomaly they returned to the spot to take another picture but nothing untoward was seen.

...the image looks like a World War II soldier

So what explanation can there be for the dark figure that appeared in the couple's first snap. Perhaps we are looking at the back of a menu board that the old woman is viewing from the front. The reason it wasn't present when they returned could be that the restaurant had closed and the board removed. There are restaurants, ice cream sellers and even a butcher in the area, all of whom could conceivably use such a board. One noticeable aspect of the image is that the anomaly is the darkest object in the whole photograph – it contains the blackest blacks.

Figures That Shouldn't Be There

Many ghost pictures simply feature a person that shouldn't be there, or indeed couldn't be where they are because of the location. We also have photographs featuring people who are not recognised by anyone present at the event in question, and when the event is something small like a birthday party held in a private house, things start to get mysterious.

One possible explanation of this type of photograph is a phenomenon known as photographer blindness. This is where the photographer is so busy concentrating on the camera settings or making sure everyone is looking at the camera that they don't see something happening in the frame right in front of them. It's not until the picture is viewed at leisure that the aberration emerges, usually to the mystification of all present.

When you're taking a photograph and everything is ready its usually a good idea to have a last scan around the frame before the button is pressed – just to make sure a marching band hasn't wandered into frame whilst you were getting Auntie Ethel to smile. And in case you're feeling smug thinking that sort of thing would never catch you out – have you seen the video of the two teams passing a basketball between themselves? Did you try to count the number of passes between those wearing white shirts, and if so, did you see the gorilla? Suffice to say, it is easy to miss the blindingly obvious when you are concentrating on something else.

Having said that it's both easy and lazy (although sometimes correct) to simply dismiss ghost photographs as something the photographer didn't spot at the time and as stated in the introduction, for the purposes of this book, I am taking the photographers' explanations of the photographic circumstances as truth and a direct record of the events. Therefore, if they say there was no one there, there was no one there.

For some images it's not just the fact that there shouldn't be a figure but that there couldn't be a figure. There are plenty of locations that we can see but for various reasons can't actually get to. There might not be access, or in some cases there may be just a shell of a building, yet in the picture we see someone looking out of a second-floor window when we know there isn't a second floor to stand on. This chapter features a collection of photographs all united by the presence of figures that shouldn't be there.

Caught on the Stairs

This photograph was taken at Agua Calientes in Peru. It's the closest modern habitation to the ancient ruins of Machu Picchu, so as spiritual and emotive locations go, you can't get much better. The photographer woke up early in the morning, excited at his imminent trip to Machu Picchu and decided to take a few photographs of the hotel – impressed or bemused as he was by the lack of a roof.

When he looked at the photograph he was curious about the mysterious object he had just captured. And no, it's not the streak of light moving up through the photograph; it's the image on the stairs – quite a distinct shady figure walking down.

The photographer is convinced the shape of the top of the head is that of an ornate headdress and he says he can also make out a necklace and some blood on the leg. He describes the streak of light as an energy bolt that looks like a double helix.

The streak of light is easily explained. The photograph was taken early in the morning when it was not yet fully light. As the camera has been exposed for the low-light levels, the shutter has remained open for a relatively long time and the photographer has not realised this. After he has pressed the shutter-release he has moved the camera down, not knowing the shutter is still open, and this movement has recorded the bright street light as part of the image.

So that explains the light, but then there is still the figure...

...it's the image on the stairs – quite a distinct shady figure walking down

Ghost in the Next Room

Shown here is an early pair of low-resolution digital photographs. The two boys are the photographer's grandchildren and both pictures were taken close together. For those who think they are the same photograph with subsequent digital manipulation, they are not. There are small differences between them as can be seen by the boys' facial expressions – it's a case of 'I've got a new camera, let me take a few pictures to try it out'.

In the first picture everything is normal: two boys pose for their grandfather; there is a glass window behind them allowing light into the hallway beyond the room where the photographs were taken. In the next

...someone else has appeared. There's a woman looking in through the hallway window

photograph a few seconds later, someone else has appeared. There's a woman looking in through the hallway window. Now let's be honest, you usually know when there's someone else in your house, but the photographer is sure that no one else was present and furthermore, no one involved with the family recognises the woman.

When you look at the picture the woman is behind the vases rather than superimposed over them. She can't be standing in the hallway as material is visible through her. If she was a reflection, she must have been in the room with everyone else, but all are adamant there was no one else. To try to ensure there were no stray reflections – perhaps of someone walking past outside – the photographer and his family have tried every possible scenario to replicate it, all to no avail. However, there have been earlier photographs (mainly Polaroids) that have also shown extra people...

I Can See You

Opposite is a nice photograph of a family house, a former parsonage, where the family in question had lived for 15 years when this picture was taken. When the photograph was viewed on a computer an apparent image of a child was seen in the bottom left window. The only other person present was the photographer's mother and she was in the house. So intrigued were the family that they showed the photograph around and a paranormal investigation team asked permission to visit. When they did they managed to produce some electronic voice phenomena (EVP) recordings. An audio recorder is left running while questions are asked and a gap is left between each question. The theory is that in the gaps it is possible to hear messages answering the questions when the tape is played back. So is this a ghost photograph with audio evidence to back it up?

Of all the photographs examined as part of the *Hauntings: the Science of Ghosts* event this was the one that provoked most discussion. Some labelled it the most amazing photograph they had ever seen, others claimed rather than a child the figure has a beard and moustache. Some suggestions were that it is a reflection, a plumber, a happy accident of placement of objects that look human, a deliberate fake, and others even saw several spirits in the picture!

...is this a ghost photograph with audio evidence to back it up?

Impression of a Ghost

A husband and wife visiting Monet's Garden in Giverny, France, do the usual tourist thing – take photographs on the bridge overlooking the famous lily pond. Two pictures were taken of the wife standing on the bridge, one with a digital and one with a film camera. The difference between the two is the time it took to put one camera down and pick the other one up.

The photographs were both taken when the bridge was relatively empty and yet on the digital version there is the figure of a woman standing next to the wife. It should be noted that the film version also has two individuals at the opposite end of the bridge. Both photographer and subject are convinced there was no one standing next to the wife as the photograph was taken.

...there is the figure of a woman standing next to the wife

The figure, which is quite clear, appears behind the hanging vines, so we're not seeing random shapes interpreted as a figure or digital manipulation. Many observers have concluded the clothing is Edwardian. It has also been pointed out that the woman and her clothing bear more than a passing resemblance to the 1873 painting *Wild Poppies Near Argenteuil,* by a certain Claude Monet. If photographer and subject are correct and no one else was around, were they visited by one of Monet's models?

Gaudi's Ghost

Gaudi's cathedral in Barcelona (the still unfinished Temple Expiatori de la Sagrada Família) is an inspiring location at the best of times, so throw in a ghost and you can't go wrong! This couple had taken the lift to the top for the views and then decided to walk down the stairs for the exercise. Just before reaching the ground they took this photograph.

The area is not accessible to the public, hence the bars. The location is the area where the cathedral bells are rung. The figure in the top middle segment was not present when the photograph was taken, only when it was subsequently viewed.

Shadows extend from the patch of light but none seems the cause of the monk-like figure

Shadows extend from the patch of light but none seems the cause of the monk-like figure. Someone has suggested we are looking at the shadow of a gargoyle, but the object looks too solid for that. Whatever it is, it is intriguing and seems the perfect excuse for a trip to Barcelona! There is only one person buried in the cathedral and that is Gaudi himself, and he is not known for wearing monkish robes.

Waiter, More Spirits Please

This is a photograph of the first group of people to arrive at a graduation party. They maintain that there was no one standing next to them when the photograph was taken, however, at a graduation party you are unlikely to know everyone present so perhaps it is no surprise the face of the ghostly image is not recognisable to them.

There is plenty of evidence that this photograph has been taken in night-mode. The colours in the foreground are harsher and colder than those in the background, as is the light from the flash compared to the warm colours of the bulbs in the fluorescent tubes illuminating the walls from above. The subjects show redeye – light reflecting from the back of the eye through the large pupil; this only happens with flash because if the ambient light were brighter, the pupils would be smaller and we would not see this effect.

...it is no surprise the face of the ghostly image is not recognisable

The evidence of a long exposure is that the wall and background details show motion blur, so the camera must have been moving. In fact most of the subjects show signs of movement. In particular, we have another party guest who has paused and moved on – he is not still long enough to produce a solid image and as we look at the photograph, we can see the trail of his drink moving as a dark blur towards the image edge.

Spirits in the Beer Cellar

This photograph was taken in the damp cellar of the King Charles II pub in n Ross on Wye, England, as the pumping equipment was moved to a drier part of the building. It was shown around so people could see what the beer cellar had been like. One day, as the photograph was being shown, someone enquired about the man standing on the left? No one had noticed him before. And of course, when the photograph was taken the photographer was by himself.

A bit of local research showed that the King Charles II pub cellar was part of a tunnel that had been used to transport prisoners. The negative of the picture was investigated and as far as anyone could tell there had been no tampering at that point. The live-in manager in the 1980s reported all sorts of unexplained happenings, including barrels moving around and gas supplies constantly being turned off. Several other occupants have detailed similar occurrences and two psychics, who carried out investigations, gave comparable accounts. Some have pointed out the figure would have to be very tall to gain this position in the photograph. If it is a genuine ghost, he may be standing on the old floor level that has subsequently changed.

...the King Charles II pub cellar was part of a tunnel that had been used to transport prisoners

The photograph was featured in the local paper but the press photographer (James Watkins) had great difficulty in compiling material for the article – curious marks kept appearing in the area of the figure, no matter how he adjusted the equipment. Watkins said he had never encountered anything like it. The pub is still there, so there is still a chance to have a pint amongst the spirits!

A Water Spirit

This is another photograph where no one saw anything when it was taken and the anomaly wasn't noticed until a long time afterwards. In fact, the photograph was being used as a desktop background on a computer when someone enquired who the second figure on the left was.

When the picture is enlarged a girl with a ponytail, wearing shorts and a t-shirt, and who appears to be washing her feet, is visible. The image is sharp; the figure is clear but transparent and she also seems to have an unhealthy grey pallor. The anomalous figure is more blurred than the subject and does not appear on any other photographs taken at the same time. Suggestions that the image is a combination of shadows and sticks that just happen to look like a figure and give a reflection that also looks like a figure, do seem to be stretching it a bit!

The subject of the photograph is crossing in one of the only safe places in the area, at most other locations the water is knee deep. For extra ghost evidence, there used to be a bridge near this spot and there are said to have been several suicides that took place there. Finally, for added value, over the right-hand shoulder of the anomalous figure a smiling face is staring out at us!

...over the right-hand shoulder of the anomalous figure a smiling face is staring out at us

Ghost on the Jetty

On a trip to the beach at Hastings on the south coast of England, the photographer decided that a photograph of a boat was the order of the day, but when a friend viewed the picture they noticed something more. On the right-hand side there is a pier and at the end of the pier there is a large, white figure. The pier is incomplete, so for a person to get there, whilst not impossible, would not be just a case of walking along the pier. The figure is not clearly in focus as it was not intended to be the subject of the photograph.

...at the end of the pier there is a large, white figure

The shadows are in the right location, the figure seems solid and to be wearing long white robes. The white blobs along the pier are presumably seagulls, so this gives us an idea of scale. If correct, the figure is twice the size of a normal person but doesn't appear to scare the birds!

If you were to visit the location, however, all would be explained because you will find a navigation aid at the end of the pier. It's a white structure about 3 metres tall with a ladder up one side and a solar panel on the other; it is the solar panel that can be viewed as the 'arm' on the right-hand side of the image. This photograph just goes to show not only how important it is to visit areas where paranormal pictures have been taken but also how easy it is to miss objects in a photograph when you're concentrating on something else.

Fishing From Blackpool Tower

This is a photograph taken a few years ago of Blackpool Tower, England's most-famous seaside landmark complete with a person sitting on the edge of the tower with a bag and fishing rod. However, knowing the size of the tower the 'fishing ghost' would be around 3 metres tall.

The photograph has been taken at night, so in low-light conditions. Even if it fired, a flash would not help, as it would be too far from the subject. The only light for this picture is the ambient light and that from the tower itself, which can be seen clearly illuminated. Looking at the lights on the tower there is definite camera movement, either down and to the right (most likely) or up and to the left. This movement pattern matches the orientation of the image. The light source is not the bulbs illuminating the tower but most likely that from the lift as it ascends to the top of the tower.

...knowing the size of the tower the 'fishing ghost' would be around 3 metres tall.

Ghost at the Door

For any technophile readers I believe this is the only photograph in the book to be taken on the film format APS (a film smaller than 35mm that might have caught on more if digital had not entered the scene). The photograph is of the side entrance to a church in France and a figure can be clearly seen in the middle, possibly holding something such as a candle or even a cartoon-style bomb!

There is something strange about this doorway when we look closely at it. There is a surround of white stones, then inside this border, where the door should fit, there is more brickwork; and when we get to the door, it is placed off centre. The door also has an odd flatness to it. (This last point is just an impression as this is a scan of a photograph and as such, is not perfect.)

It almost looks as if this is a painting of a door rather than an actual door and that this is covered with a pane of glass. This pane is then reflecting a figure, creating an illusion known as 'Peppers Ghost'. However, the more I look at the image the more uneasy I feel – the shadows are not what I would expect. On the extreme right there is a shadow where the wall coming towards us meets the brick wall, suggesting a gap. Then there is a shadow on the doorframe but it's on the left – a flash would illuminate it so that all the shadows were on the same side. A curious photograph for many reasons and I think a visit to the location is called for.

...a figure can clearly be seen in the middle, possibly holding something such as a candle

Heads Up – It's a Ghost

This chapter has been compiled simply as a result of the large number of photographs I collected that seem to show a head by itself, or in a couple of cases, a body sadly lacking a head.

One thing that always amazes me about ghost reports is that someone will see a headless ghost and then confidently report it as (for example) the ghost of Anne Boleyn. How do they know?

There are a number of portraits of Anne Boleyn, so we know what she looked like, so someone seeing her ghost might be able to identify her from pictures, but how can you identify a person, probably unknown to you, from their headless body?

If headless ghosts do exist then how can you tell the difference between Anne Boleyn and any other similarly dressed woman of the time? Anne Boleyn wasn't the only Tudor woman to have her head chopped off. She wasn't even the only wife of Henry VIII to be beheaded. In some cases the key is in the location – for example, a headless ghost in Tudor garb at Hampton Court is more likely to be Anne Boleyn.

There are so many unanswered questions with headless ghosts. Why are they headless? Why aren't they reunited with their heads in the afterlife? How does a headless ghost navigate? They weren't walking around headless when they were alive so why should they be doing so now? This brings us nicely to the other aspect of this chapter – appearances just of heads. Do they belong to the headless ghosts but are they doomed to haunt by themselves? If so, how do they get around? Again, why would we see a head without a body if they weren't like that in life? We may ask, what is a ghost and what do they symbolise? Do they represent a person as they were in life, or at a traumatic time in their lives, or at their point of death?

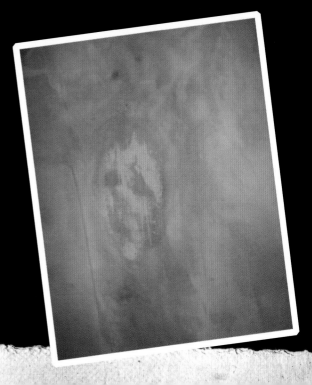

Poster Poser

Here are two friends photographed in the Barcelona Metro, standing in front of a perfectly ordinary advertising poster, except the head of the central character in the poster is a little strange; it is illuminated differently to the rest of the photograph and it has an ethereal glow.

Rather than a ghost photograph, I think what we have here is a picture reflecting light from the camera flash. Many advertising posters in metro and tube stations use shiny paper and ink. When the flash hits the reflective surface it can come straight back at the camera causing an area of overexposure on the resultant photograph. The mysterious face it could be seen as a negative of how the face should look – the black ink is more reflective than the base material, so it reflects more light. But why is it just the face? This is because of relative angles – light travels in straight lines but the surfaces of the metro tunnel and poster are curved. It is also being viewed at an angle so only light from that exact spot (by coincidence) is being reflected back to the camera. Light would also be reflected from other areas but would only be picked up in this overexposed way by cameras in different positions. A nice effect though!

The mysterious face could be seen as a negative of how the face should look

Head Trip

This is a photograph taken on a Canadian road trip as the travellers stop off for an evening's rest. The phantom is quite clear in the bookcase on the right-hand side – no vague suggestions of an image here. The photographer and his friends call this shot 'Matt and the Head', and the head seems to look like Matt but without his glasses. Now if there's no natural explanation such as a Matt-mask, what are we looking at?

Some people will see this picture and scream out that it's been digitally manipulated, but having looked at the image under magnification there is no sign of this. Also, a look at the metadata shows the image is exactly as it was first shot. It is possible the image could have been created and then re-photographed, but there are no signs of this either.

If it's a ghost of Matt then it's a ghost of a living person

Quite clearly the position is such that no living person could get into that space. If it's a ghost of Matt then it's a ghost of a living person, and whilst such things are reported, they are normally regarded as a crisis apparition. (A crisis apparition is alleged to appear before a person's death but Matt did not die after this picture was taken.) Could it be a thought form (an image created by people thinking about it), a doppelganger (an exact double of a person – some say that meeting your own is a precursor to your death), or a ghost that just happens to look like Matt…

125

Haunted Snowman

Only one comment was submitted with this photograph and I repeat it in its entirety: 'See the "ghostly" image of the girl to the right of the snowman.' There was no further elaboration and I think the use of quotation marks on the word 'ghostly' tell a tale.

When we look at the picture the ghostly image is to the right of the snowman but when looking left of the snowman we see exactly the same girl. It is possible it is her twin sister poking her head through a gap but the face seems too opaque for that.

Listening to people discuss this picture, I've heard talk about things such as reflections and so on. If it were a reflection, it is probable that other elements of the image would also be reflected, but there is no evidence of this. Additionally, if it were a reflection the two images would be identical apart from aberrations caused by the reflecting material, for example, distortion caused by a drop of water. However, the two faces are not identical – the hair is different and on the main image the mouth is open whereas it is closed on the ghostly image.

My instinct is that this is a photograph that has been constructed by computer software – cutting an image from a different photo, pasting it into the relevant area and changing the translucency to make it a bit see-through.

See the 'ghostly' image of the girl to the right of the snowman

The Ghost in the Well

This image was taken looking down a well in a rural French village. The well had a lid that is held open as the photograph was taken. At one point the photographer thought she saw something strange but couldn't quite define it, so continued taking pictures. Subsequently, this image was found on one of them – a grinning demon face is staring up at us from the bottom of the well.

It is most likely that ripples caused the image – perhaps the result of a combination of a small stone dislodged from the top of the well, the reflection of light and clouds from above, with the human brain filling in the rest. However, others have pointed out that water has long been used for divination purposes and mediums have often claimed to see faces and other images reflected in it.

...a grinning demon face is staring up at us from the bottom of the well

Other photographs taken at the time clearly show the arm of the person holding the lid up and no mysterious face. Even this reflection from the top of the well is quite indistinct because of the distance from the top to the bottom. A flash was also used to take the picture and this is seen to a degree illuminating the sides of the well.

The Ghost in the Wall

A former army officer plastering a bedroom wall for his partner discovered a face in the plaster. The face stayed for two weeks before the plaster dried, and even when the wall was papered over, the outline of the face was still present, although the features had disappeared.

Two photographs of the face were taken in rapid succession and between them the whole colour of the picture changed. Instead of the expected grey of the plaster, the image had a blue tint. As well as the plaster taking a long time to dry and the face to fade, it is reported that this room is constantly cold.

Given the propensity of the human brain to join the dots and see faces, is this what we have here? Or does the spirit world interact with the living world simply by rearranging things that are already there?

...the outline of the face was still present, although the features had disappeared

It's also possible that the digital camera was confused by the greyness of the wet plaster. Most digital cameras have an auto-white balance where, for example, the scene is analysed to make sure there is no colour cast due to different types of lighting. It may be that the reflectiveness of the damp plaster caused the camera to misinterpret the scene. It has also been pointed out that the plasterer responsible should not give up the day job!

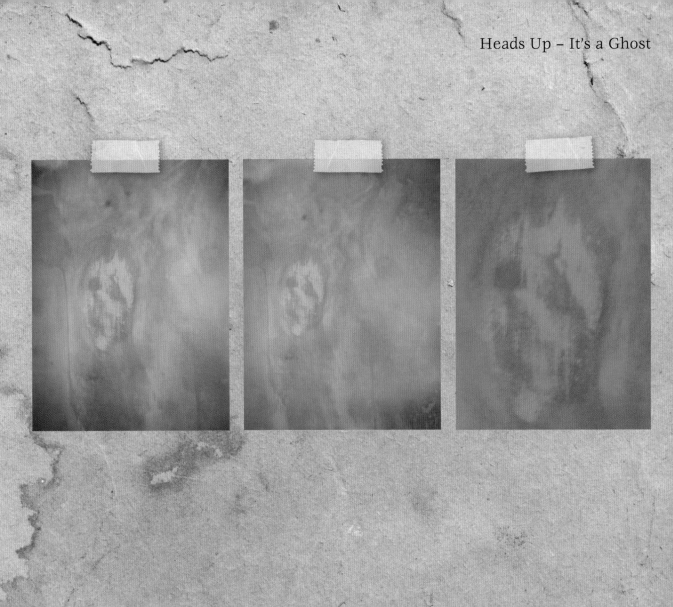

The Ghost Behind the Wall

This is possibly the oldest picture in this book, however it hasn't been widely distributed. Prior to it being taken, the house was always described as having an atmosphere and being spooky, and it had a history of young women dying there.

The uncle of the girl photographed took and developed the picture, and when her parents saw it, they immediately spotted the face in the background peering over the fence. The face was also present on another photograph taken the same day.

The mother asked that he never show the picture to the girl, so it wasn't until many years after the mother's death that he dared to show it to her. The girl was captivated by it. Every time she looked at it she could see the face more clearly and by enlarging it, the face was clearer still. From knowing the location and looking at apparent positions, the family worked out the face must be only a few inches across, but no one was able to identify it.

Every time she looked at it she could see the face more clearly and by enlarging it, the face was clearer still

Viewers of the photograph fall into two camps: those who believe it definitely is a ghost and those who think it is just the arrangement of leaves that our minds interpret as a face. Regrettably, the second image taken from the same position moments later sheds no further light on its reality or otherwise.

Headless Ghost in the Galleries of Justice

Here is a photograph of the Galleries of Justice in Nottingham, central England. In the centre is a doorway: on one side there is a mannequin and on the other side of the entrance is the figure of an alleged ghost, a headless ghost no less. Interestingly, there is no corresponding mannequin on this side.

The Galleries of Justice have reportedly been the location of a number of paranormal happenings and ghost investigations over the years, and it has a reputation for being haunted. Enlarged prints from the original photograph seem to show an even more obvious body shape.

Paint splashes have been suggested as an explanation for the image, but surely in a location such as this they would be removed very quickly. Reflections in the varnished wood is another suggestion but these would be more diffused – we can see an example of this on the left-hand side where it has no shape other than a blob of light, whereas the alleged ghost has the appearance of a figure hunched over.

...on the other side of the entrance is the figure of a headless ghost

The Ghost in the Water

This is another example where the photographer (the children's mother) doesn't think the picture shows a ghost putting it down to a coincidence that produced a ghostly apparition. Over the shoulder of the little girl a face can be seen in the water. Some have described it as skeletal, others see a moustachioed and bespectacled gentleman.

A close look at the patch of water shows it could be an underwater rock with ripples and light scattered in different directions. It may even be caused by a duck!

Is this a perfect example of how good the human mind is at making sense from random patterns of nothingness? The mother might not be convinced it's a ghost but the grandmother is and she describes how she reacted when she first saw the photograph as 'jumping out of my skin'!

Some have described it as skeletal, others see a moustachioed and bespectacled gentleman

Family Gatherings and Parties

One thing guaranteed to bring out a camera is a family gathering. For many the full-clan get together is a rarity, so they are generally recorded for posterity. These can range from joyous occasions such as christenings, birthdays and weddings, to the more sombre, such as funerals. For some it may seem strange to take photographs at a funeral, but for many it is a rare chance to see relatives.

As well as family gatherings I have also included Christmas parties and general work outings, so essentially this is a chapter about get togethers and photographs taken in the process.

Some pictures produced such confusion in those present that they returned to the location to seek a solution. In some cases they have gone as far as interviewing local people who could explain the comings and goings of the area.

If, as some believe, the appearance of a spirit is triggered by an outpouring of emotion (the theory is that the energy released is used to make the spirit materialise), parties and gatherings that surely raise emotional levels provide the

ect opportunity for this to happen. However, if that is
case, why don't we see more ghosts at events such as
tball matches?

e particular photograph in this chapter has been doing
rounds for years. Someone must have originally taken
ut was it the person who submitted it, or if it was found
line, is the story purely fabricated to accompany it?

The Smallest Bridesmaid and Her Ghostly Friend

Taken quite a few years ago, here is a wedding photograph that was submitted by the smallest bridesmaid in the shot (who is now grown up). At the time the picture was taken she recalls feeling very sad and cold, and she could not move. When she saw this photograph she noticed the white figure to the extreme left described by her as being like a little girl with a veil over her head. She has returned to the location a number of times since and spoken to the vicar about the photograph and one thing is clear – in that location there has never been a gravestone, fence or seat, thus ruling out the obvious explanation of misinterpretation of these common objects.

One non-paranormal explanation would be a fault with the camera's wind-on mechanism. This is a photograph taken on a film camera, probably some sort of instamatic. Once one photograph is taken, the film has to be manually advanced ready for the next. It was possible with these cameras to take a picture immediately after another without advancing the film, but this would produce two images on the same negative. It was also feasible to partially advance the film, allowing part of a second photograph to be superimposed on the first negative. An examination of the negative would help solve the mystery if this were the case.

...she recalls feeling very sad and cold, and she could not move

Office Party Gate-Crasher

This photograph shows a staff Christmas party with a gate-crasher at the extreme right-hand side. The figure is very different to the two girls, so it's not a double exposure of their image as the hair parting and other characteristics are clearly different.

As with many other photographs in this book, the photographer is adamant there was no one else present, so we can rule out someone leaping into the photograph at the last second, or a third individual moving whilst the photograph was taken.

Behind the girls is a wall, so anyone attempting to jump into the photograph would have had to take a very circuitous route and would have been noticed by all present. However, when other members of the party saw the photograph no one recognised her.

...when other members of the party saw the photograph no one recognised her

Erm, Who Are You?

Holding the baby is the grandmother and looking on is the mother to the extreme right. In between them is a face that no one recognises. A number of other photographs were taken the same day and none show anyone who should not be there. Whoever it is seems to be solid. The grandmother is casting a shadow from the flash onto the face and the head itself is casting a shadow towards the background. The noses of the woman holding the baby and the mysterious image are different when examined under high magnification, as are the hairstyles. Therefore, it is not the same woman exposed twice on the film.

In between them is a face that no one recognises

If it were a double exposure other areas of the picture would show some evidence and there is none. If this were a digital image we could say it was pixelated because we can clearly see the dots that make up the image but being taken in 1987 it must have been taken with a film camera. The excessive grain could be from a small film format which has been over enlarged (such as the 110 format), or it could be an incorrectly exposed photograph that has been printed and shows poor picture quality. To get technical, an underexposed negative that has been deliberately overexposed in the printing process gives a viewable image but accentuates the film grain, making it difficult to properly assess an image. The face is too clear to be a placement of objects interpreted as a face, besides the photographer is adamant there was no one there and no one present recognises the individual. Clearly a mystery...

Most Likely to Be a Ghost – the Top Five

As mentioned in the introduction, some of the images in this book were submitted as part of the *Hauntings: the Science of Ghosts* event which was part of the Edinburgh International Science Festival. As part of this exhibition there was an online participatory event where members of the public were invited to submit their own ghost photos for inclusion on a website. Visitors to the site were then invited to vote on whether they thought the photographs were faked, genuine, had a reasonable explanation or were uncertain.

Out of the 300,000 or so people from around the world who voted, we selected the top five photographs that people felt were most likely to be real ghosts and these are presented in this chapter.

Out of these top five photographs, the photographer of one of the images did not believe he had caught a real ghost, but over 30 per cent of voters did!

Another of the pictures prompted people to sort through their albums to find similar photographs and one surfaced that had been taken 30 years earlier (*see page 78*).

Another was taken in the decidedly non-haunted location of a side street as the photographer took a shot to use for an advert to sell his car.

The remaining two photographs show a grey, misty figure walking in front of a couple being photographed and a ghostly fisherman looking out to sea.

Together they make a chilling collection of ghost photographs. What do you think?

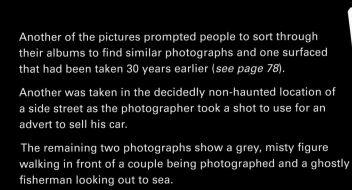

It's Not a Ghost

Here is a photograph that the photographer did not feel was a ghost but 31 per cent of those voting did! John Wilson was out walking with his children and the family dog when he paused to take a photograph near an old Victorian mine. John commented, 'I am not a ghost kind of person and so I think it's most likely just shadows and branches coming together to look spooky. Still creepy though,' he admits.

Our brains are hard-wired to make sense of random patterns and in particular, faces and figures are very important to our interpretation of the world. A classic example of this is the ability to discern faces and patterns in such random objects as clouds or in the flames of a fire. This phenomenon, paradolia, commonly explains photographs of this nature. It is also an easy way to dismiss something that may actually be there.

...there seems to be a greenish face floating from left to right

Some have likened the face in the bushes to *The Scream* by Edvard Munch. It has also been pointed out that there is, surprisingly, another ghostly figure in this photograph: just to the left and above the girl's head there seems to be a greenish face floating from left to right; a hand is visible as well as what appears to be a light shirt under a dark coat. Therefore, is this a case of paradolia with an actual ghost for good measure, or two incidents of paradolia in the same picture, with the second not being seen by the original photographer?

Car for Sale – Ghost Passenger Thrown in for Free

When Guillermo Sosa decided to sell his car, the last thing he expected to see was a ghost. Guillermo had planned to sell his car online and so needed a photograph to advertise it. As he prepared his advertisement, he noticed something a little strange – the reflection of a face in the driver's side wing mirror. But that was impossible. There was no one in the vicinity when the photograph was taken.

If you look closely, you will see that the face looks quite large. Objects in car mirrors are always closer than you think, so to produce an image of this size, the person would have had to have been very close indeed.

Guillermo is not aware of any accidents with previous owners of the car, and he has not had any accidents with the car himself. Some have claimed that the picture has been doctored in Photoshop, but there is no evidence of this. The photograph was originally shot on film and the print was subsequently scanned for the advert. Therefore it is impossible to determine if the image has been manipulated because Guillermo used Photoshop to prepare the advert, so who knows if the reflection of the figure was added at the same time. Others claim that the reflection is merely the back rest of the seat, however this explanation seems a little far fetched. The image does seem to resemble a face and a back seat reflection would look much more like, well, a back seat!

...the last thing he expected to see was a ghost

Late Night Walking Ghost

Unusually the ghost in this digital photograph was spotted in the camera immediately after it was taken rather than when the photographs were downloaded at home. Mathieu Fur was out for a late night walk with five friends when they paused to take a photograph. Two people were in front of the camera and the remaining four were behind it. However Fur is adamant that no one walked in front of the camera when the picture was being taken.

The picture was taken on a slow shutter speed. We know this because in the top right of the photo there is a white, comma-like shape, which is a street lamp. This shape is the result of movement of the camera or 'camera shake'. Depending on the camera and focal length of the lens used, it can be difficult to hold a camera steady at fractions of a second longer than about 1/30th of a second.

...the ghost in this digital photograph was spotted in the camera immediately

This photograph was actually taken at a setting of one second, which means that there was plenty of opportunity for camera shake. And plenty of time for a person to walk in front of the camera and leave a blur on the resultant image. But why didn't Fur notice this at the time? Perhaps, knowing the camera would be open for a long time, he was concentrating on holding it as steady as possible and, having set up the initial composition of the scene he may no longer have been paying attention to it. Could it be that by the time he had finished and returned his attention to his friends, the mysterious stranger had moved on?

Ghostly Fisherman at the Rock and Spindle

To the east of St Andrews on the east coast of Scotland is the Rock and Spindle rock formation. The circular spindle in the centre of the photograph is basalt rock that cooled in a cavity with the vertical distaff (or rock) the last remnants of a lava tube. Over the years erosion of the surrounding rocks has exposed the structure that the more romantic liken to a spinning wheel.

Out for a walk on a chilly day Chris Brown and his son paused for a photograph, and as is often the case, it was not until the photographs were examined on a computer that an unexpected image was seen. To the right of the spindle there is a dark figure looking out to sea. It can almost be imagined the figure is waiting for someone to return from a long sea voyage. The longer you look the clearer the figure becomes, but what we have here appears to be nothing more than a cave and its reflection in the surrounding sea. (The cave is another part of the erosion that produced the famous landmark.)

To the right of the spindle there is a dark figure looking out to sea

That seems to end the matter except for one small detail. Twenty years before this photograph was taken, another shot was supposedly produced showing a figure in this same cave wearing a green anorak, boots and standing in the sea. Upon subsequent investigation a piece of green cloth with a zip was found in the cave. Unfortunately I have been unable to track this picture down.

A Ruff Day at Tantallon Castle

Photographer Chris Aitchison was visiting Tantallon Castle on the east coast of Scotland in 2008 when, as all good tourists do, he took a photograph of the central keep, standing inside looking upwards. When he got home he downloaded the day's photographs to his computer and it was only when he was looking through them that he noticed a figure, not present at the time the photograph was taken. The figure seemed to resemble an Elizabethan woman, complete with ruff.

Unlike some locations, Tantallon Castle does not feature costumed guides, nor are there mannequins in period costume illustrating the life of the castle. Aitchison was so intrigued with the single image that he contacted the castle to ensure that there were no enactments happening that day. There were none.

The photograph appears to show a figure (possibly a woman) in a ruff coming down the stairs. Some have even suggested that it is the ghost of King James V of Scotland who owned the castle between 1529 and 1542.

The figure seemed to resemble an Elizabethan woman

Others have suggested that the apparition may have been caused by sunlight glinting on some rocks in the stairwell. The light appears to be coming from the top left of the photograph and, as there is no roof on the central keep, it is possible that the light was shining in and just at that moment it happened to fall on a piece of exposed masonry.

The location of the figure is accessible by the public – it is part of a stairwell leading to the upper floors and the west tower (Douglas Tower) – so it is possible that we have simply a photograph of a tourist walking down the stairs. But if that's so, why is she wearing what does indeed distinctly look like an Elizabethan ruff?

Acknowledgements

This section of a book is traditionally used to thank those without whom the book would not have happened, so who am I to fight tradition.

I would like to thank Richard Wiseman and Caroline Watt, along with Simon Gage OBE of the Edinburgh International Science Festival.

I would also like to say 'thank you' to all the photographers who have allowed their pictures to be used in this book.

This is starting to sound like an Oscar speech but I'd like to thank John Barron for nurturing my love of photography, my wife Alison Rutter and my mother Kathleen Dixon just for being themselves and for their love and help throughout the years. And Charles Fort should get a mention somewhere too.

Finally, a big thanks to all those very nice, helpful folk at David and Charles who made this such an easy process, in particular Neil Baber and Sarah Callard.

Picture Credits

The photographs used in this book have come from many sources and acknowledgement has been made wherever possible. If images have been used without due credit or acknowledgement, through no fault of our own, apologies are offered. If notified, the publisher will be pleased to rectify any errors or omissions in future editions.

6, 136 © Desiree Lafontaine; 6, 103 © Paul Sicuro; 8, 138, 142 © Richard Poulton; 9, 86 © Elaine Handley; 10, 14 © Mark Stocks; 11, 27 © RAB; 11, 19, 20, 23, 24, 28, 30, 35, 43, 48, 51, 55, 67, 89, 99, 115, 121, 131, 139, 141, 145, 148 © Unknown; 13 © Diane Moore; 17 © Janey Lee; 29, 33 © Peter Morton; 29, 40 © Edmir Branco; 36 © Natogue; 39 © Lindsay Beadnell; 45 © Anon; 46 © Lesley Stringer; 49, 70 © Gill Hutton; 49, 61 © Liz Smith; 52 © Sue Newton; 56 © Gordon Rutter; 59 © Danny Davis; 62 © Matthew McGurn; 65 © Lorraine Morrison; 69 © Neil Smith; 72, 95 © Dominic Lane; 73, 79 © Kelly Jane Lamb; 73, 93 © Eric Walker; 75 © Gillian Steele; 76 © John Field; 81 © Ashley Whitham; 82 © Suzanne Stafford; 85 © Belen Patricia Alvarez; 89 © Benjamin Lovegrove; 90 © Victoria Hatch; 96, 118 © Martin Hulm; 97, 109 © Patrick Valentin; 97, 113 © Jamie McCloud; 101 © Ben Forsdike/Ken King; 104 © Ian Robertshaw; 107 © Urshulette Toerien; 110 © Anon; 115 © William Blake; 116 © Lyndsay Foreman; 120, 129 © Nicole Morgan; 121, 127 © Enver Buzoku; 122 © Gaeten Alzieu; 124 © Tony Hill; 132 © Sarah Flannery; 135 © Paul Shortland; 147, 150 © Guillermo Sosa; 147, 153 © Mathieu Fur; 147, 155 © Chris Brown; 156 © Chris Aitchison

Index

GHOST CHRONICLES
Stories of the Paranormal
ISBN 978-0-7153-3779-0

Three spooky volumes of classic real-life ghost stories that will make your hair stand on end.

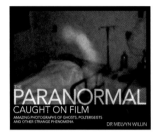

THE PARANORMAL CAUGHT ON FILM
Dr Melvyn Willin
ISBN 978-0-7153-2980-1

A fascinating compendium of paranormal phenomena presented by leading expert, Dr Melvyn Willin.

MONSTERS CAUGHT ON FILM
Dr Melvyn Willin
ISBN 978-0-7153-3774-5

A mysterious and mesmerizing collection of photographs depicting monsters and incredible creatures from around the world.

GHOSTS CAUGHT ON FILM 2
Jim Eaton
ISBN 978-0-7153-3202-3

From shadowy figures, strange mists and apparitions to angels and demons, *Ghosts Caught on Film 2* is a compendium of extraordinary phenomena captured on camera.

LOVED THIS BOOK?

Tell us what you think and you could win another fantastic book from David & Charles in our monthly prize draw.